Cat Home Alone

Fifty Ways to Keep Your Cat Happy and Safe While You're Away

Cat Home Alone

Fifty Ways to Keep Your Cat Happy and Safe While You're Away

Regen Dennis

**Andrews McMeel
Publishing**

Kansas City

www.andrewsmcmeel.com

Cover and box design by Two Pollard Design
Interior design by Heidi Baughman
Illustrated by Kipling West
Edited by Alison Herschberg

ISBN: 0-8362-3259-3

From the *Cat Home Alone* packaged set, which includes a cat toy and this book.

Cat Home Alone is produced by becker&mayer!, Ltd.

ATTENTION: SCHOOLS AND BUSINESSES

Andrews McMeel books are available at quantity discounts with bulk purchase for educational, business, or sales promotional use. For information, please write to: Special Sales Department, Andrews McMeel Publishing, 4520 Main Street, Kansas City, Missouri 64111.

Dedication

To my mother, Mary Katherine MacDonald, cat-sitter extraordinaire, who lovingly spoils her grandcat with handmade toys and tidbits of salmon.

Introduction

Do you find it wrenching to leave for work with your favorite feline companion's bereft little face pressed against the window—or, worse still, looking mischievously toward your Lalique collection? Cats left alone for long periods of time quickly invent lots of ways to cope with loneliness, from rampant destruction to listless overeating. Still, cats are the perfect companions if you work outside the home or travel frequently. They're independent and relatively self-sufficient, and perfectly capable of creating their own fun with the simplest of toys, such as curtains, houseplants, electrical cords, or crystal vases.

With a little creativity and planning, you can keep Kitty busy and happy while you're gone. Cats have very basic needs: food and water, a litter box, sumptuous comfort, and zillions of things to play with. Using a few diversionary tactics, you can transform your home or apartment into a virtual kitty playground without sacrificing your human needs. You'll rid yourself of virtually every vestige of guilt while you're at work or cruising on the Mediterranean.

Cats thrive on surprise, so try each of the ideas in *Cat Home Alone* one at a time. Once Kitty is on to a game, that game is over and it's time for a new one.

From now on, when you come home from work or a weekend trip, your house won't have that freshly shredded look. Kitty will have lost his feelings of abandonment and maintained his self-image as the center of the universe, and you can finally stop worrying and feeling guilty. You'll both find life less stressful and more fun. Take it from your cat: Life is a game!

Playtime and Exercise

1. Kitty Tetherball. The cat toy included in this kit will give your cat hours of fun—and exercise. Simply clip it to a doorjamb or a piece of sturdy furniture, making sure there's adequate room for long-distance pounces, sneak attacks, pirouettes, thrusts, and parries.

2.

Create a Kitty Disneyland in your home while maintaining a facade of normal housekeeping. Strategically placed dangle-toys, empty boxes, and catnip-stuffed mousies will surprise and entertain your cat during those boring interludes between naps.

3. Rotate Kitty's arsenal of toys. Never leave the same toys out for more than a few days. Store some of the toys in a jar filled with catnip. When favorite toys magically reappear, they'll seem like completely new adventures. Surprise Kitty with new toys by leaving them where he can find them, near his favorite napping place or on the way to the food bowl.

4. Kitty Batting Practice. Attach a soft toy, preferably one with a bell, to an elastic cord and suspend it from a doorknob or from the top rung of a ladder-back chair, so it hangs a few inches off the floor. Dare Kitty to walk by without swatting it.

5.

Occasionally leave a plain cardboard box—just slightly larger than your cat—on the floor when you leave. Kitty will immediately possess it as his very own and store special toys there or crawl in for a cozy nap.

MI CASA MI ES ~~MI~~ SU CASA!

6. Open a paper shopping bag and leave it in the middle of the kitchen floor just before you leave for work. Kitty will have a great time zooming in and out, hiding and sleeping in the bag. For an extra treat, sprinkle a generous pinch of catnip in the bag.

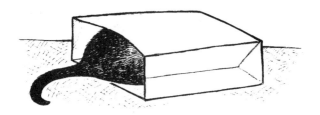

Dining and Drinking

7. Fill Kitty's bowls with food and fresh water before you go to work each day. Staring at an empty bowl could trigger an eating disorder or similar emotional trauma.

8. An automatic-feeder bowl allows Kitty unlimited—and unscheduled—munching when you're gone for more than one day. Pour in a few days' worth of meals, and she'll be content knowing dinner's always ready.

9. If your cat shares her living space with a dog, find a special, secure place for her food bowl. Try the top of the refrigerator or dryer, where Woofer can't reach it.

10. Most cats learn early that drinking out of the toilet bowl is clever and practical. If you keep your bathroom reasonably clean, it's probably not a health hazard. But if Kitty's precarious balancing act on the toilet seat makes you crazy, keep the lid down!

11.

Prop up a mirror behind Kitty's food bowl, and she'll think she has company for lunch.

Personal Stuff

12. Clean out Kitty's litter box every night, and change it once a week. If the litter gets smelly and soiled, he will deem it disgusting and may decide not to use it anymore.

13.

When you're away on a trip, include "Clean litter box" at the top of the daily checklist for your cat-sitter. If you've left Kitty on his own for a few days, a big scoop of baking soda mixed into the litter will help eliminate some litter-box odor.

Sleeping Places

14. Place a big, soft pillow on the floor by a picture window (and a heating vent, if possible), so Kitty can meditate about the meaning of life while watching the world outside—in the warm, sumptuous comfort she deserves.

15.

Create places where she can snuggle and burrow—a down quilt tossed across a bed, an open dresser drawer full of cashmere sweaters, an heirloom afghan on the couch. Cats thrive on opulence.

16.

Wherever possible, use fabrics with lots of texture for Kitty to sleep on: smooth satin, soft angora or mohair, an old fur collar, your new full-length mink coat—all are special treats for little paws.

17.

Pet stores carry wonderful carpeted cat condos and climbing perches, from the simple to the exotic to the utterly decadent. Of course, some cats delight in shunning any product specifically designed for feline use. But if Kitty can get past that and accept the made-for-her concept, put her new throne in a quiet place where she'll feel safe.

18.

Indoor cats might enjoy a window hammock, available at many pet stores and through catalogs. These are essentially fabric platforms that attach to window frames. Kitty can enjoy the security of a high perch, nap by a sunny window, and watch the birds go by.

Securing the House

19. Your priceless collection of Zuni fetishes, crystal wine glasses, or hand-carved candlesticks is a tantalizing target. Unless your precious objects are unbreakable, move them out of Kitty's reach or display them behind glass. Nothing—repeat *nothing*—is safe when you're away.

20. Be aware that when you walk out the door, the rules leave with you. The forbidden kitchen counter suddenly becomes irresistible, especially if the butter dish is out. Self-discipline is not Kitty's strong suit.

21. Creatively arranging the garbage all over the kitchen floor satisfies Kitty's penchant for artistic expression. Remove temptation by emptying discarded delicacies, such as fish or meat scraps, that produce really fabulous aromas.

22.

Study your home security system, and adjust it so your cat can't trigger the alarm. Cats spend countless hours calculating how to foil motion and heat sensors, and can break high-jump records to set off an alarm.

23. Ever wonder where cat burglary got its name? Adept paws crave the challenge of opening doors and cabinets. Installing a childproof latch will ensure that your garbage or pantry remains safely behind closed doors.

24.

Cats think that perching on the toilet seat and unrolling the toilet paper with both paws is great exercise and lots of fun. If you don't want to see yards of toilet tissue in a fluffy pile on the bathroom floor, secure the roll with a rubber band.

25. Before you leave for work, make sure taboo playthings are secure: rubber bands, paper clips, cotton balls, ponytail fasteners. Otherwise, don't expect to find things as you left them. In fact, don't expect to ever see them again, at least until you move the furniture for spring cleaning.

Gardening for Cats

26. Some cats excel at indoor gardening and do their best soil work while you're away. If African violets, Christmas cacti, or exotic cyclamens are your cat's hobby, either move them to a place where Kitty can't reach them (good luck) or keep them in a room with the door shut.

27. Grow Kitty's own recreational drugs! Catnip is an easy and attractive perennial in the garden or in a small pot, and if Kitty doesn't mow it to the ground early in the season, it will produce attractive flowers. Cat grass looks like thick grass and satisfies Kitty's salad cravings. Tending her own indoor crops might divert Kitty from nibbling on houseplants. Bring in pots or sprigs of cat plants every five or six days. Homegrown drugs should be a treat, not a daily fix.

Step-Siblings

28. Cats make lousy pet-sitters. Leaving them on their own with ground-based pets such as gerbils or turtles is a bad, bad idea, and could prove fatal if Kitty begins having food-chain fantasies.

29. Even though Tweety is safely locked in his cage, the sweetest, most adorable cat can still terrify him—curious paws delight in poking through the bars. Just imagine the effect of having a lip-smacking cat up-close-and-personal for hours on end.

30.

The best antiboredom device for a cat is another cat. If you have the room and the psychological wherewithal to appreciate the synergistic antics and subversive plotting of two cats, adopt a playmate for your pet.

31.

Your cat has his own thoughts about the "Dogs are man's best friend" adage. If Kitty and Doofus don't get along when you're there, don't expect them to be buddies when you're gone. Make sure Kitty has safe places where he can go to get away from his canine companion.

32.

The theory that cats abhor water might be tested if Kitty discovers the fishbowl. Splashing a paw at the goldfish can be great sport—but catch-and-release is not widely honored in feline fishing circles. Keep your aquarium covered or safely displayed in a closed-off room.

High-Tech Kitty

33. Pop in a CD of nature sounds so Kitty can transport herself into the jungle. The roars of lions and tigers, and the calls of birds and other prey, will enhance Kitty's fantasy life.

34. Set a series of self-timers on lamps, radios, and the TV to create some action around the house. Lamps also generate heat for nap-time basking. Be sure the radio and TV are tuned to Kitty's favorite stations. The random sound-and-light show will also help deter potential burglars.

35.  Start Kitty's day on a high note—put a Video Catnip cassette into the VCR as you leave for work. These realistic videos of birds flying, squirrels cracking nuts, and mice doing mouse things fascinate most felines, some to the point that they'll paw at the screen. Of course, you run the risk that Kitty will become addicted to the tube or, worse still, try to get inside it.

Keeping Kitty Safe and Healthy

36. Sometimes the most basic household items bring out the highest levels of creative genius in a bored cat. Take an inventory of each room and try to second-guess the enticements it offers a cat. Stifle feline fantasies of bungee jumping by tucking away attractive electrical cords dangling from lamps, irons, or hair dryers. Quash Kitty's desire to redecorate by moving any top-heavy boxes, flower arrangements, stacks of books, or priceless bronze sculptures that are precariously placed and easily toppled. Quell your cat's spelunking urges by closing the dryer door.

37.

Make certain your cat always wears a collar with a license and an ID tag with a phone number. Clever cats (meaning all cats) can outfox you or the most conscientious cat-sitter, and if Kitty dashes outside for a major adventure, you'll want to maximize your chances of getting him back.

38.
Most cats want to be alone when they're not feeling well. And most sick kitties will do just fine while you're gone for the day. But if your cat is seriously ill—recovering from surgery or from battle wounds suffered in a neighborhood tussle— you'll rest easier if someone, preferably your kitty-sitter, can stop by to check up on him and give any necessary medication.

Addictions and Bad Habits

39. If you train your kitten at an early age to refrain from frenzied shredding of draperies and furniture, she probably won't resort to evil ways when you're gone. But if Kitty gets away with occasional scratching sprees, don't be surprised to return to a newly textured sofa.

Latchkey Cats

40. Cats whose humans travel a lot often adapt well to a shared-custody arrangement. Cat-door cats in friendly neighborhoods can be equally at home with several families.

41.

If your cat is accustomed to the easy-come, easy-go luxury of a cat door, it's not a good idea to disrupt his routine when you're away at work or even when you'll be away for a few days. With no one to play with while you're away, Kitty will appreciate the diversions of tree climbing, rodent chasing, and bird stalking all the more. Nonetheless, weigh these considerations: If Kitty gets hurt or sick, she may not come back inside, and your cat-sitter won't know what's wrong or where she is. And there is a remote possibility that other animals may decide to visit.

42. Be prepared for Kitty to welcome you home from work with gifts: formerly live birds, mice, frogs, or other trophy game. It's important that you react with delight and joy. Praise Kitty; call him the Lion King, the greatest hunter of all time. Then majestically scoop the hapless creature (the critter, not the cat) into a plastic bag and give it a respectable burial in the garbage can.

Kitty-Sitters

43. A great place to find a cat-sitter is your local Humane Society. Talk to them about their volunteers, particularly teens or seniors. These folks are almost guaranteed to adore animals and have an above-average sense of responsibility. They'll probably also appreciate a little extra money. Or check the newspapers or Yellow Pages under "Pets" or "Pet Boarding and Sitting Services." Professional cat-sitters may cost a little more, but you'll know they have experience taking care of pets.

44.

Before hiring a professional kitty-sitter for the first time, ask for references—and call them. One telephone call can buy a lot of peace of mind and help you confirm expectations, rates, and reliability. Kitty will thank you. Note: A good rule of thumb is to pay your kitty-sitter the going rate for baby-sitters in your neighborhood.

45.

Carefully review the specifics about what you want your kitty-sitter to do, and how often. This might include basics such as feeding, putting down fresh water, cleaning the litter box, and spending at least forty-five minutes, preferably twice a day, playing with your feline friend. If Kitty needs regular medication, show the sitter how to give it, and have the sitter practice with you there, just to make sure she or he understands the procedure.

46.

Prepare a list of basic information to leave with your kitty-sitter: where you can be reached, your vet's name and number, the name of any medication your cat's taking (in case Kitty hides the pill bottle), the name and phone number of a neighbor. You cannot trust Kitty to provide accurate information.

STEAK
TWICE
DAILY

47.

By expanding your cat-sitter's job to include picking up mail and newspapers, rotating light timers, opening or closing draperies, watering the lawn, or looking after any other household tasks, you'll be increasing the time the sitter and Kitty spend—and bond—together. A twenty-four-hour house-sitter is the best solution of all.

Guilt

48.
You will naturally have twinges of guilt about leaving Kitty alone all day or—God forbid—for a couple of days or more. It's important to indulge and wallow in this guilt, because Kitty would want you to feel ashamed and abashed for allowing your attention to focus anywhere other than on her needs.

49.

Allow a few minutes before you leave for work each day to get on the floor with Kitty and her toys, to brush her, or to hold her in your lap while you're reading the paper. When you leave a cat purring, you'll feel better all day, and so will your little feline friend.

50.

When you arrive home after an absence of a few days or more, don't expect the purrs and nuzzles of a warm welcome. Kitty must exhibit appropriate disdain and indifference to punish you and re-establish her household dominance. Fawning patience and groveling humility might speed up Kitty's acceptance of your apology.

60

About the Author

Regen Dennis writes for cats and children of all ages. Her most recent book, *Tarot for Cats*, has helped thousands of cats delve into the occult and unlock the mysteries of their nine lives. She lives at Muskrat Point in Renton, Washington, with her cat and her husband.